THOMAS CRANE PUBLIC LIBRARY
QUINCY MA

CITY APPROPRIATION

THE SCIENCE OF
NUTRITION

# WHY WE NEED
# VITAMINS

By Marina Cohen

## Crabtree Publishing Company
www.crabtreebooks.com

# Crabtree Publishing Company

## www.crabtreebooks.com

**Author:** Marina Cohen
**Publishing plan research and development:**
  Sean Charlebois, Reagan Miller
**Editors:** Sarah Eason, Nick Hunter, Lynn Peppas
**Proofreaders:** Robyn Hardyman, Kathy Middleton
**Project coordinator:** Kathy Middleton
**Design:** Calcium
**Photo Research:** Susannah Jayes
**Print coordinator:** Katherine Berti
**Production coordinator and prepress technician:**
  Ken Wright
**Series consultant:** Julie Negrin

**Picture credits:**

Shutterstock: cover, 8828810875 25, 33, Yuri Arcurs 42, R Ashrafov 18, Ben44 34, William Berry 39, BlueOrange Studio 14, Sandra Caldwell 28, DenisNata 6, Lev Dolgachov 20, Elena Elisseeva 4, Gelpi 30, Get4net 44-45, Mandy Godbehear 12, Karamysh 31, 38, Piotr Marcinski 17, Felix Mizioznikov 23, Monkey Business Images 13, 15, 22, 26, Aine Moorad 41, Juriah Mosin 29, Naluwan 43, Kirsty Pargeter 7, Stefanolunardi 40, Dmitry Suzdalev 27, Suzanne Tucker 32, Bo Valentino 21, Milan Vasicek 19, Vikiri 10, Visionaryft 36, Matka Wariatka 9, Ivonne Wierink 11, Buida Nikita Yourievich 8, ZanyZeus 24, Zeljkosantrac 16

### Library and Archives Canada Cataloguing in Publication

Cohen, Marina
    Why we need vitamins / Marina Cohen.

(The science of nutrition)
Includes index.
Issued also in electronic format.
ISBN 978-0-7787-1690-7 (bound).--ISBN 978-0-7787-1697-6 (pbk.)

        1. Vitamins in human nutrition--Juvenile literature.
I. Title.  II. Series: Science of nutrition (St. Catharines, Ont.)

QP771.C64 2011          j612.3'99          C2011-900211-6

### Library of Congress Cataloging-in-Publication Data

Cohen, Marina, 1967-
  Why we need vitamins / Marina Cohen.
      p. cm. -- (The science of nutrition)
  Includes index.
  ISBN 978-0-7787-1697-6 (pbk. : alk. paper) -- ISBN 978-0-7787-1690-7 (reinforced library binding : alk. paper) -- ISBN 978-1-4271-9681-1 (electronic pdf : alk. paper)
  1. Vitamins--Juvenile literature. 2. Nutrition--Juvenile literature.
  I. Title. II. Series.

  QP771.C62 2011
  612.3'99--dc22

                                                    2010052771

## Crabtree Publishing Company

www.crabtreebooks.com          1-800-387-7650

Printed in the U.S.A./022011/CJ20101228

**Published in Canada**
**Crabtree Publishing**
616 Welland Ave.
St. Catharines, Ontario
L2M 5V6

**Published in the United States**
**Crabtree Publishing**
PMB 59051
350 Fifth Avenue, 59th Floor
New York, New York 10118

**Published in the United Kingdom**
**Crabtree Publishing**
Maritime House
Basin Road North, Hove
BN41 1WR

**Published in Australia**
**Crabtree Publishing**
386 Mt. Alexander Rd.
Ascot Vale (Melbourne)
VIC 3032

# CONTENTS

# FOOD FOR FUEL

**Y**ou might not think about the food you put in your mouth, but what you eat makes a big difference to your health. Inside your food are many important **nutrients** you need to stay healthy.

## You need nutrients

The main nutrients your body needs are **carbohydrates**, **fats**, and **proteins**, but you also need tiny amounts of other nutrients called vitamins and minerals. You have to eat enough—but not too much—of each type of nutrient to stay healthy. You also need to eat the correct number of servings from each group according to your age. Luckily, each nutrient is found in many different foods, so you can choose healthful food that you like.

*Salads made with raw vegetables are full of vitamins.*

*The food pyramid shows healthy foods only. It does not include foods such as cookies and chips, which are high in salt, fat, or sugar.*

**Grains**
*Grains give you energy, but they also contain some protein and other nutrients.*

**Vegetables and fruits**
*You should eat a wide range from these two groups to get all the nutrients you need.*

**Oils and fats**
*These foods should not be overeaten.*

**Milk**
*This group of foods is rich in protein but can also be high in fat.*

**Meat and beans**
*These foods are rich in protein, although meats can also be high in fat.*

## A balanced diet

This book is about vitamins. There are lots of different vitamins. No one food contains all the vitamins we need for good health.

The food pyramid divides healthy food into six different groups. Choosing food from these groups will give you all the nutrients you need.

# WHAT ARE VITAMINS?

## Body Talk

In the late 19th century, people made an important discovery. They realized that if a person ate certain foods they did not get certain diseases. Scientists were excited. They began trying to identify these mysterious factors that are good for our health.

**V**itamins are nutrients that are present in very small quantities in our food. A vitamin is an **organic** substance. This means it is found in living things, such as animals and plants.

### Healthy vitamins

Vitamins are found in all living things, and we need them to stay healthy. Thousands of years ago, farms did not exist, so food was not grown for people. There were no grocery stores or restaurants. People spent most of their lives searching for food to stay alive. These people had no idea about proper nutrition, however, they were surprisingly healthy. They did not suffer from illnesses such as **diabetes** and heart disease.

*All living things contain vitamins.*

## Discovering vitamins

In the 1890s, a Dutch doctor, Christiaan Eijkman, noticed that chickens that ate nothing but white rice—rice with the dark skin removed —got sick. He noticed, too, that if he fed the dark skin to the sick chickens, they got better. This was a great stage in the discovery of vitamins.

In 1912, a Polish scientist named Casimir Funk read about Eijkman's discovery. Funk then managed to isolate the mysterious ingredient from the skin of brown rice. He called it a "vitamine," because it contained an amine group—a nitrogen **atom** connected to two hydrogen atoms. Since not all vitamins contain amine groups, the word was shortened to "vitamin" a few years later.

## Did you know?

Cooking and baking often destroys vitamins—so eating a slice of apple pie is not the same as eating a fresh apple! And do not forget to eat your peel. There are more vitamins in the peel of apples, potatoes, and lemons than in their flesh.

*I never knew about vitamins until I started food technology class at school.*

*Eat the peel of fruit along with the flesh for a healthy hit of essential vitamins.*

## Types of vitamins

There are two basic groups of vitamins: water-soluble and fat-soluble vitamins. Within these two groups, there are many different vitamins. Each of these vitamins can be found in different types of foods and does a different job in the body.

### Did you know?

There are eight B vitamins. When scientists first discovered the B vitamins, they thought they were all the same vitamin. Research then proved they were different vitamins found within the same foods.

## Water-soluble vitamins

As their name suggests, water-soluble vitamins dissolve in water. Your body cannot store water-soluble vitamins. They travel around in your blood. If your body does not use them all, they leave through your urine. These vitamins must be replaced often.

Water-soluble vitamins are easily destroyed during food storage and preparation. By keeping fresh fruit and vegetables in the fridge, and milk and grains out of the light, they will not lose as many vitamins.

*I love eating fruits. They taste great and are packed with loads of vitamins.*

*Eating a juicy orange is a good way to get the vitamin C your body needs.*

# Body Talk

These tables show the chemical names of some common water-soluble and fat-soluble vitamins:

## WATER-SOLUBLE VITAMINS

| Vitamin | Chemical name |
| --- | --- |
| Vitamin C | Ascorbic acid |
| Vitamin B1 | Thiamine |
| Vitamin B2 | Riboflavin |
| Vitamin B3 | Niacin |
| Vitamin B5 | Pantothenic acid |
| Vitamin B6 | Pyridoxine |
| Vitamin B7 | Biotin |
| Vitamin B9 | Folic acid |
| Vitamin B12 | Cyanocobalamin |

## FAT-SOLUBLE VITAMINS

| Vitamin | Chemical name |
| --- | --- |
| Vitamin A | Retinol |
| Vitamin D | Cholecalciferol |
| Vitamin E | Tocopherols |
| Vitamin K | (various) |

## Fat-soluble vitamins

Fat-soluble vitamins do not dissolve in water. They are stored in your fat cells and in your liver. They can hang around in your body for a long time. This means you do not need to get as much of them. It also means your body cannot get rid of them as easily as water-soluble vitamins.

*Keeping fruits and vegetables in the fridge helps to preserve the vitamins in the food.*

# WHERE ARE VITAMINS FOUND?

**A**ll living things contain vitamins, but different plants and animals contain different vitamins. To get all the vitamins your body needs, you need to eat a wide variety of healthy foods every day.

**Vitamin-rich fruits and vegetables**

Some vitamins are only found in plants. Vitamin C is a very important part of our diet. It is commonly found in fruits and vegetables. Fruits and vegetables are also good sources of other vitamins. For example, leafy greens, such as spinach and parsley, contain vitamin K. Asparagus, broccoli, cabbage, soybeans, avocados, and kiwi fruit are also good sources of this important vitamin.

Green leafy vegetables contain vitamin E. Raw sunflower and pumpkin seeds are also excellent sources of vitamin E. So too are vegetable oil, almonds, and avocado.

*Kiwi fruits are packed with vitamin C.*

## Did you know?

Beta-carotene is an organic substance found in some plants. Our bodies convert beta-carotene into vitamin A. Sweet potatoes, carrots, mangos, cantaloupe, and dried apricots are full of beta-carotene. It is what gives them their orange color.

## Body Talk

You are not only what you eat—what you drink counts as well! Drinks such as milk and fruit juice contain vital vitamins that your body needs to stay healthy.

*I eat plenty of vegetables to make sure I get enough vitamins each day.*

*Eating carrots will give you a healthy dose of important vitamins.*

## Vitamins in animals

Animals are also a good source of the vitamins we need to stay healthy. Oysters, other shellfish, and liver contain vitamin B12. Milk and eggs also contain vitamin B12.

Some people are strict vegetarians. They do not eat meat or anything that comes from an animal, such as milk or eggs. Since vitamin B12 is only found in animal foods, strict vegetarians must take a B12 supplement.

*Hanging out in the sun is an easy and relaxing way to get vitamin D.*

### Body Talk

Tiny living things, called **bacteria**, are living on and inside your body. Some bacteria are harmful and can make you sick, but most of the bacteria in you are harmless—or even helpful. Some bacteria found inside your **intestines** can make two very important B vitamins: biotin and pantothenic acid. When certain chemicals inside the bacteria react to one another, they are converted into more complex products such as biotin.

*I love eating sushi. It tastes great, and it is full of vitamins and other nutrients.*

*Sushi is a healthy snack, and it is easy to make.*

## Did you know?

Sushi is a Japanese dish. It consists of rice mixed with vinegar and is topped with ingredients such as raw fish. Sushi rolls are wrapped in pressed seaweed. Seaweed is an excellent source of vitamin K.

## The sunny vitamin

Vitamin D is an interesting vitamin because we get it from sunlight. When rays of natural sunlight touch your skin, your body makes its own supply of vitamin D.

Vitamin D is also found in foods such as salmon, mackerel, tuna, and mushrooms, but it is impossible to get enough of this vitamin just from food. You need sunlight to top up the level of vitamin D in your body. Staring out the window will not work! The glass blocks out the rays that help you produce vitamin D.

# HOW MANY VITAMINS DO WE NEED?

Our bodies only need very small amounts of each vitamin, but all vitamins are equally important. Too much or too little of a particular vitamin can lead to serious health problems.

*Eating a range of foods from an early age will give you all the vitamins and other nutrients your body needs to grow.*

## Body Talk

Smoking is one of the unhealthiest habits anyone can have. Smoking is linked to cancer, heart disease, stroke, bronchitis, high blood pressure—the list goes on and on. Smoking also robs your body of vitamin C, folic acid, thiamine, and vitamin B6.

## Recommended Dietary Allowance (RDA)

During WWII, the U.S. National Academy of Sciences came up with a set of daily requirements for each nutrient, depending on a person's age and gender. This Recommended Dietary Allowance, or RDA, is still used as the basis for setting the current Recommended Daily Intake, or RDI.

## How much is enough?

It is especially important that babies, children, and teens get proper nutrition so they can grow into healthy adults. Because their bodies are growing and developing rapidly, they may require more vitamins—in relation to their size—than adults.

As you get older, your body becomes less able to absorb nutrients, so seniors may require more vitamins to stay healthy. Pregnant women also need extra vitamins to provide their own bodies, as well as their developing **fetuses**, with the proper nutrients.

*Pregnant women need a balanced diet to make sure their babies are born healthy.*

*I never used to like eating vitamins. But now I know how good they are for you, so I eat lots and lots.*

## Did you know?

Vitamins are measured in units called milligrams (mg) or micrograms (mcg). These are very small quantities. That is why food experts refer to vitamins as micronutrients.

## Body Talk

Sunscreen protects your body from the harmful effects of sunlight, but it also stops your skin from making vitamin D. It is important to get enough sunshine, but not too much.

## Too many vitamins are bad for you

Too much of some vitamins can make you sick. This is especially true for fat-soluble vitamins. Your body can store fat-soluble vitamins for up to six months. Since our bodies cannot get rid of them as easily as water-soluble vitamins, too much of a fat-soluble vitamin can cause health problems.

## Too much vitamin A

Too much vitamin A can give you headaches and nausea. It can even make you lose your hair! Your appetite is your physical desire to eat or drink. It is your body's way of telling you you need energy. Too much vitamin A can actually make you lose your appetite. You cannot get too much vitamin D by staying out in the sun for too long. Within about 20 minutes, vitamin D reaches a balance in your skin, so the body simply gets rid of any further vitamin D that is produced.

*Too much sun can burn your skin and lead to skin cancer, so it is wise to use sunscreen.*

## Can you have too many B vitamins?

Your body usually gets rid of any excess B vitamins in your body by flushing them out in your urine. But sometimes a person might get too much vitamin B6 in his or her body. If this happens, it can damage the nerves in the arms and legs, making the person feel numb.

*Too much vitamin A can give you a headache and make you feel sick.*

*I tried sunbathing all day to get more vitamin D, but I just got sunburned!*

## Did you know?

Pantothenic acid is a B vitamin that helps your body make **hormones**. Hormones are chemicals that act a little like messengers. They travel through your body in the bloodstream, sending information to your tissues and organs. Too much or too little pantothenic acid can affect your hormones. In turn, this can affect your growth, development, and your mood.

## Too few vitamins are bad for you

If your body lacks a particular vitamin you have a vitamin **deficiency**. A vitamin deficiency can be caused by not eating enough of the right foods. Some diseases can also prevent your body from absorbing enough vitamins.

## Scurvy—the sailors' scourge

Scurvy was one of the first illnesses to be identified as being related to nutrition. It is caused by a lack of vitamin C. Native North Americans came up with the first cure for scurvy —a tea made from boiled tree bark containing vitamin C.

In 1749, a Scottish surgeon named James Lind found out that limes prevented scurvy. Sailors often died of scurvy since they had no fresh fruit and vegetables at sea. After the discovery, the British Royal Navy made sure their boats were stocked up with limes.

I put lime and lemon juice on my salads. It tastes delicious.

*A grapefruit for breakfast is a good way to get a healthy dose of vitamin C.*

## Pellagra

Pellagra is a disease caused by a lack of niacin. The name comes from the Italian meaning "sour skin." People suffering from pellagra get sores all over their skin.

## Beriberi

In 1884, a Japanese medical doctor named Takaki Kanehiro noticed that people who ate nothing but white rice got a disease called beriberi. This illness damages the nervous system and can be deadly. Today, we know that beriberi is caused by a lack of thiamine in the body.

### Body Talk

When you go for a checkup, the doctor will often ask you to stick out your tongue. If it looks shiny and swollen, and tiny red bumps on your tongue shrink or even disappear, you have something called smooth tongue. This can be caused by a lack of vitamins, including folic acid.

*A healthy-looking tongue is a good sign that you are getting enough vitamins. A healthy tongue should be pink and moist.*

## Did you know?

You need to eat foods with plenty of water-soluble vitamins to replace those lost in your urine.

## Body Talk

People who suffer from a disease called cystic fibrosis cannot absorb vitamins and other nutrients very well. This leads to poor growth and development.

### What causes anemia?

Dark leafy vegetables, fish, and citrus fruits such as oranges, lemons, and limes are all high in folic acid. If your body does not get enough folic acid, you could develop a health problem called anemia. Anemia happens when your body does not produce enough red blood cells, making you feel tired all the time.

> My sister has anemia. It is really bad. She sometimes finds it hard to get out of bed.

*If you have pale skin and feel tired all the time, you might have anemia.*

## What is pernicious anemia?

Some people have an illness called pernicious anemia. This disease prevents the body from absorbing vitamin B12. A lack of vitamin B12 may cause mental health problems, such as dementia and depression. Dementia refers to several conditions in which the brain stops working properly.

## The importance of fat-soluble vitamins

Your body can store fat-soluble vitamins, but you can still have a deficiency. Too little vitamin A can cause you to have a condition known as night blindness. This is when a person's eyes have trouble adjusting to dim lights. Rickets is a disease caused by a lack of vitamin D. Rickets causes your bones to become soft, leading to fractures and even deformity.

*You need vitamin A for healthy eyesight.*

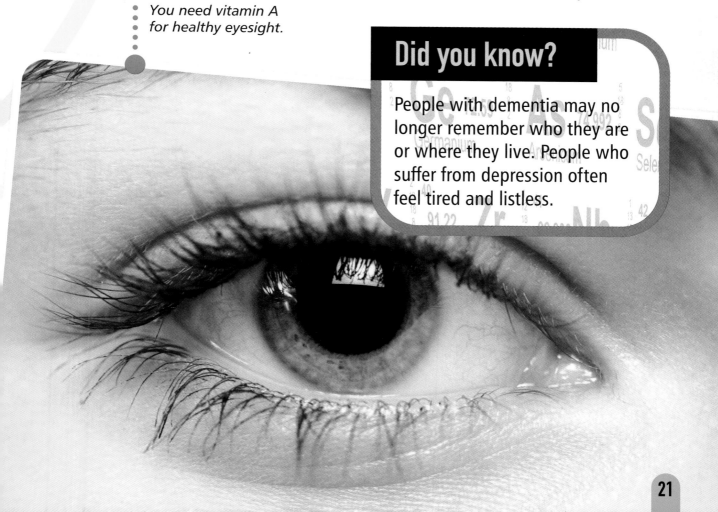

### Did you know?

People with dementia may no longer remember who they are or where they live. People who suffer from depression often feel tired and listless.

# IT'S ON THE LABEL

The table of contents at the beginning of this book tells you what is inside the book. A nutrition label tells you what is inside the food you are about to buy from a store and eat.

## What does the label tell you?

The nutrition label tells you what is in your food and how much of the main nutrients and some important vitamins and minerals it contains.

The list of ingredients on a food label gives the biggest ingredient first and the smallest ingredient last. The nutritional value of the food is also given. Beside each nutrient you will find the amount of the nutrient contained in one serving of the food. Nutrient amounts are either measured in grams (g) or milligrams (mg).

*Always check the labels on packaging to see what nutrients the food contains.*

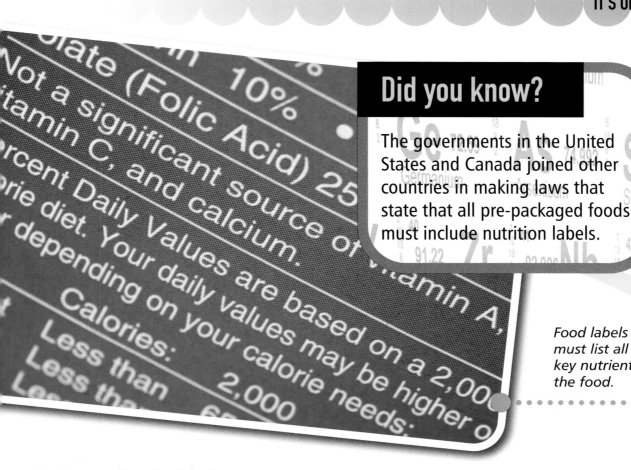

ate (Folic Acid) 25
Not a significant source of vitamin A,
itamin C, and calcium.
rcent Daily Values are based on a 2,00
rie diet. Your daily values may be higher o
depending on your calorie needs:
Calories: Less than 2,000
Less than

*Food labels must list all the key nutrients in the food.*

## Understanding the label

Food experts know just how much of each nutrient your body needs each day. The percentage Daily Value (DV) on a nutrition label tells you what percentage of the Recommended Daily Intake (RDI) of the particular nutrient you are getting in one serving of this food.

For example, one serving of one type of food may give you 20 percent of the RDI of vitamin C. This means you would still have to get the other 80 percent of vitamin C your body needs that day from other foods.

## Body Talk

Nutrient labels are calculated based on the needs of an average adult—not the needs of children. Children may need more or less of some nutrients because their bodies are still growing.

## What is a serving size?

If you look at a box of crackers or a container of soup, the nutrition label does not give you the nutrient value for the entire box or container. It refers to one serving. The label will tell you just how much of a food product is considered to be one serving. It could be four crackers, two cookies, or one cup of cereal.

Sometimes the label tells you how many grams or milliliters are in one serving of a product. If one serving of soup is four fluid ounces (125 ml), and there are eight fluid ounces (250 ml) of soup in the entire can, you need to use your math skills to figure out just how many servings there are in the can: $8 \div 4 = 2$ servings $(250 \div 125 = 2$ servings$)$.

*My dad eats much bigger servings, so he must be getting more vitamins from his food than me.*

*How many 3.5 ounce (100 g) servings are in your bowl of breakfast cereal?*

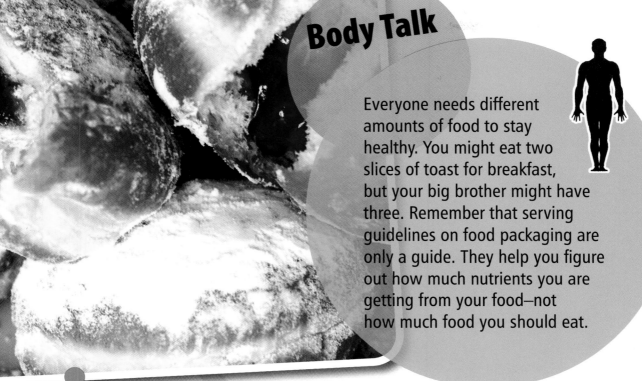

## Body Talk

Everyone needs different amounts of food to stay healthy. You might eat two slices of toast for breakfast, but your big brother might have three. Remember that serving guidelines on food packaging are only a guide. They help you figure out how much nutrients you are getting from your food—not how much food you should eat.

*A jelly donut is fine as a treat once in a while, but too much sugary food is bad for you.*

## Why label food?

The aim of food labeling is to help people make healthier food choices. You can use the nutrition labels to find out if you are eating too much of a certain food, for example, three servings instead of one. You can also use the label to compare foods to see which are higher in minerals, vitamins, and other nutrients and which are lower in **calories** and fat.

## Did you know?

Ingredients are listed in order of how much is contained in the food. Check different food labels to see where sugar is on the list! (You might see other words for sugar, such as fructose, corn syrup, and glucose.) Eating too much sugar is bad for your health, so avoid foods where sugar is high on the list.

# WHAT DO VITAMINS DO?

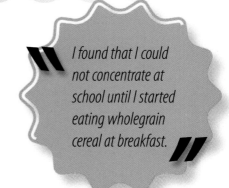

*I found that I could not concentrate at school until I started eating wholegrain cereal at breakfast.*

**O**nce you understand the important role vitamins play in being healthy, you can start to understand many of the reactions that are constantly taking place inside your body.

**What do water-soluble vitamins do?**
B vitamins help make the chemicals inside your body react with each other inside your cells. This chemical reaction is necessary for your cells to live, grow, and make new cells.

*All vitamins help keep you healthy so you can grow and stay active.*

## Getting energy from food

Do you get confused easily? Do your muscles feel weak? Then pass the peas or have a bowl of lentil soup! Or you could try spreading some liver pâté on wholegrain crackers or chewing on a pork chop. All these foods are high in vitamin B1—thiamine.

Thiamine helps release the energy from the food you eat. It also gives you a healthy appetite and is important to your nervous system. Other B vitamins also help to release energy from food.

## What does riboflavin do for you?

Riboflavin (vitamin B2) promotes healthy skin, nails, and hair. Riboflavin eases the strain on your eyes and also boosts your **immune system** by helping your body form antibodies.

Antibodies are proteins in your blood that destroy harmful germs that may have entered your body.

## Body Talk

Riboflavin helps you stay alert. So have a great riboflavin-rich breakfast before you take an important exam!

## Did you know?

If you are not getting enough riboflavin, your body will tell you. You may develop cracked or sore lips. Your eyes may feel itchy and seem very sensitive to light. You may even notice that you are shedding more hair than usual.

*Shiny, healthy hair is a sign you are getting enough riboflavin from your food.*

## Body Talk

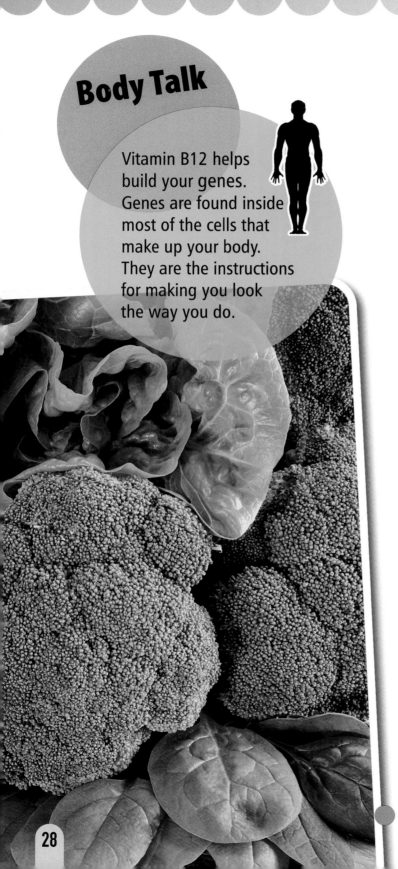

Vitamin B12 helps build your genes. Genes are found inside most of the cells that make up your body. They are the instructions for making you look the way you do.

### Do not let nerves get to you!

Are you feeling nervous or anxious? Try a tuna sandwich on wholegrain bread for lunch. Hate seafood? Have some liver or chicken instead. All these foods are high in vitamin B3—better known as niacin. Niacin helps your nerves stay healthy. It also looks after your skin and your digestive system.

### Made by folic acid

At one time you were a single, microscopic cell. Then that cell divided into two cells, which then divided into four—and so on, and so on, until you became the 30 trillion-celled person you are today. During the very early stage of your life, vitamin B9 (folic acid or folate) was playing an important role in your development.

Folic acid helps to prevent certain birth defects of the spine and the brain. Even after you are born, your body continues to need folic acid. It helps you form red blood cells and also helps you break down proteins.

*Leafy green vegetables, such as broccoli, lettuce, and spinach, are a great source of folic acid.*

> I used to be a fussy eater, but now I try different foods to get all the nutrients my body needs.

*Eating healthy tuna sandwiches is a great way to get some of the niacin and vitamin B6 your body needs.*

## B6—the protein processor

Vitamin B6 (pyridoxine) helps you break down proteins. Protein is found in foods such as meat and nuts. The more protein you eat, the more vitamin B6 your body needs. B6 also helps your body make red blood cells.

## Did you know?

Sunlight robs food of its B vitamins. If milk stands in sunlight for two hours, it will lose 60 percent of its vitamin B content.

## Body Talk

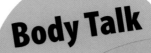

Are your bones sore? Do you bruise easily? Is your skin dry? Try eating an apple, or have a stir-fry with lots of peppers. Throw in some broccoli and potatoes for an added boost of vitamin C. You are less likely to suffer from aches, bruises, and dry skin if you eat these foods.

### Vitamin C for perfect health

Vitamin C is vital for healthy blood vessels, bones, and teeth. This is because vitamin C is needed to form collagen, a substance that is essential for growth and healing parts of the body.

*If you want healthy, shiny teeth eat plenty of foods containing vitamins C and D.*

## Absorbing vital nutrients

Vitamin C helps your body absorb other important nutrients such as iron. Beef has plenty of iron, so if you eat a hamburger, make sure you have a slice of vitamin C-rich tomato on it, or have an orange for dessert.

## What do fat-soluble vitamins do?

Fat-soluble vitamins do many different jobs to help keep your body healthy. They can help your body make new cells, and they can also help prevent diseases.

## Building up bones

Vitamin D can do some pretty amazing things. The main job of vitamin D is to help your body absorb important minerals called calcium and phosphorus. Your body needs calcium and phosphorus for healthy bones and teeth.

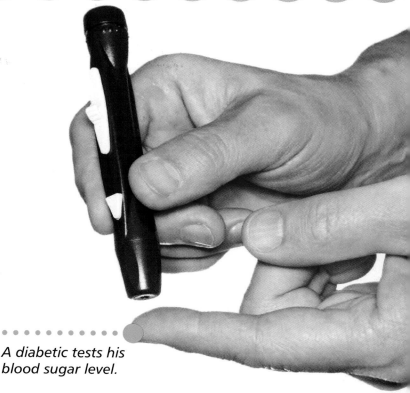

*A diabetic tests his blood sugar level.*

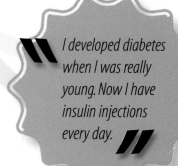

*I developed diabetes when I was really young. Now I have insulin injections every day.*

## Did you know?

Vitamin D can help prevent osteoporosis. This disease usually affects people as they grow older. It makes the bones become less dense, and they can break more easily. Vitamin D can guard against depression and even certain types of cancer. It gives your immune system an added boost and maintains your blood pressure. It helps your body make **insulin**, which prevents diabetes.

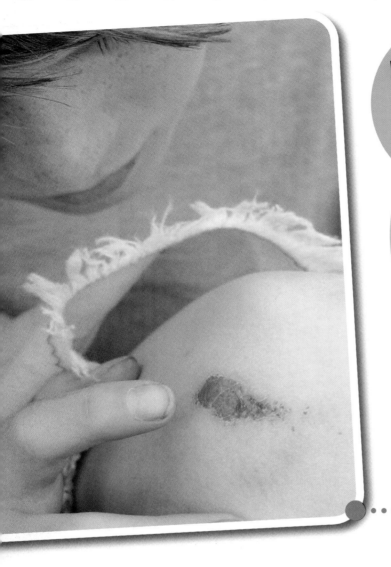

**Antioxidants** are substances that destroy **free radicals**. Everyone has free radicals in their bodies, but factors such as stress, illness, and too much sunlight can produce an excess of these harmful substances in the body. Too many free radicals can damage your cells and even cause diseases such as cancer.

*If you scrape your skin, vitamin K helps your blood clot in order to stop your body from losing too much blood.*

## How can you see in the dark?

You are lying in the dark. Someone switches on the light. A million dots swarm in front of you—this is vitamin A hard at work to help your eyes adjust to change in light. Vitamin A is essential for good vision. It also helps keep your skin and mucous **membranes** moist and healthy.

## Healing and protecting

Vitamin E helps your wounds heal and your blood circulate. Vitamin E eases muscle pain and protects your skin from the harmful effects of sunlight. But, most importantly, vitamin E is a powerful antioxidant that protects your cells from damage by harmful substances.

## Clotting your blood

If a bucket springs a leak, the water continues to pour out until there is none left. When you cut yourself, your blood flows from your wound. What stops you from bleeding to death? The answer is blood **clotting**. Vitamin K is important because it helps your blood clot and stops the flow of blood.

Vitamin K also helps your body absorb calcium. According to recent studies, it may also help in the treatment of cancer. Although most people get enough vitamin K in a normal diet, this vitamin is often given to newborn babies.

### Did you know?

Before major surgery, patients are often given extra vitamin K to help their wounds stop bleeding.

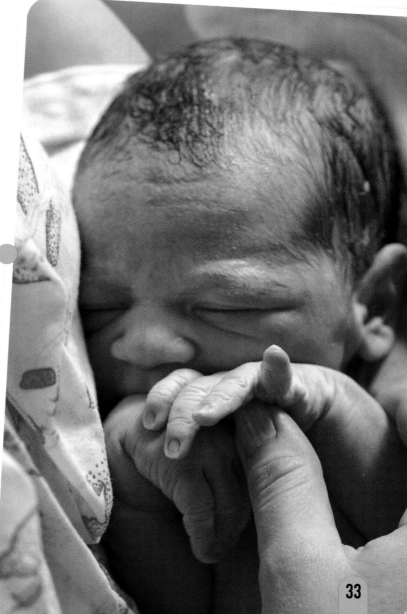

*Newborn babies often get an injection of vitamin K as a precaution to protect them from a rare form of bleeding.*

*My baby sister had a vitamin K injection when she was born.*

# DIGESTION

**A**part from vitamin D and biotin, your body cannot produce vitamins on its own. You need to get vitamins from food. But how does your body get the vitamins out of the food and send them where they need to go? It all begins in your digestive system.

## Your mouth

If you smell, see, or even think about food, **saliva** forms in your mouth. When you take a bite, your teeth break down the food into smaller pieces. Then the saliva gets to work. It helps break down the chemicals in your food. When the food has turned to mush, your tongue pushes it toward the back of your throat.

## Your esophagus

A long tube, called the **esophagus**, runs from the back of your throat down to your stomach. Once food enters the esophagus, muscles in the walls of the tube squeeze the food down into your stomach.

*Biting into a sandwich begins the digestive process.*

## Your stomach

Muscles inside your stomach mix and churn the food into smaller pieces. Gastric juices inside your stomach break down the food into a partially digested liquid called **chyme**.

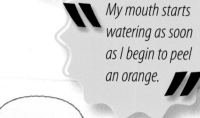

*My mouth starts watering as soon as I begin to peel an orange.*

*The food we eat passes down a tube called the esophagus into the stomach. The partially digested food then moves to the small intestine. The walls of the small intestine absorb most of the nutrients in our food. The waste then passes through the large intestine and out through the **rectum**.*

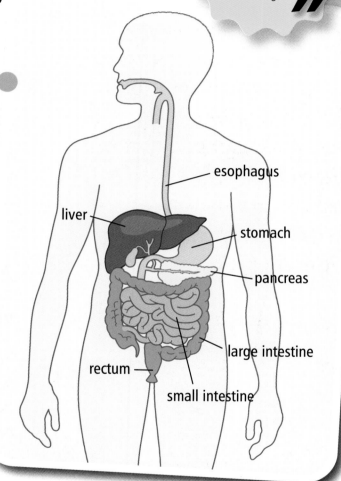

esophagus

liver

stomach

pancreas

large intestine

rectum

small intestine

## Your small intestine

Your small intestine is packed tightly under your stomach. Chyme from your stomach spends about four hours in the small intestine and is broken down into a watery mix. All the nutrients, including the vitamins, can then pass into your blood.

## Your liver

Your blood heads straight to your liver where nutrients and waste are sorted. Your liver can send vitamins where they need to go and can even store some for future use.

## Did you know?

You are made up of between 30 and 50 trillion cells! There are hundreds of different types of cells inside your body. You have skin cells, bone cells, blood cells, and brain cells—even hair cells. Each cell is very important and performs a special task.

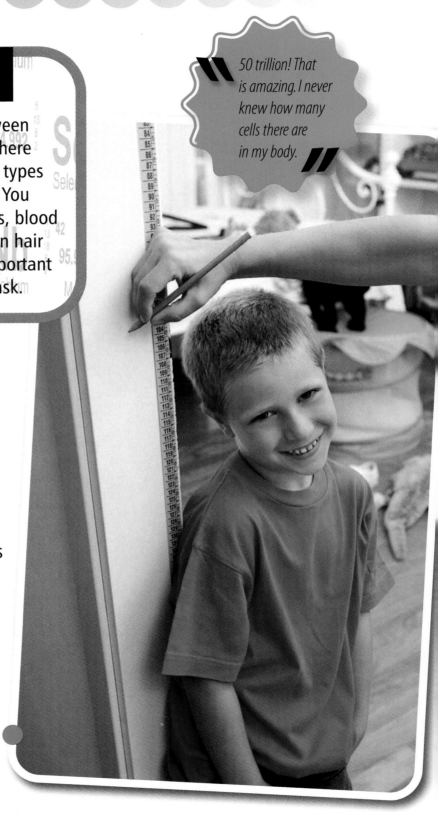

*50 trillion! That is amazing. I never knew how many cells there are in my body.*

### Vitamins and body systems

As food passes through your digestive system, water-soluble vitamins are absorbed through the walls of the small intestine and into the bloodstream. Blood constantly circulates around your body. It carries vitamins and other nutrients, along with water and oxygen, to all the body's cells. Your cells are alive, and they need nutrients to grow.

*Your body grows by making new cells. You cannot make healthy cells without vitamins.*

## What happens inside cells?

The outer layer of a cell is called the cell membrane. Once food has been broken down into tiny **molecules**, it can enter the cell by passing through the cell membrane. Carbohydrates and fats are turned into energy within cells. B vitamins are responsible for helping the cell make this chemical change.

## How do vitamins help cells grow?

Fat-soluble vitamins are responsible for other chemical changes inside cells. They help your cells stay healthy, grow, and reproduce. Fat-soluble vitamins are digested in the same way as other vitamins, but they are carried around the body by the **lymph system**.

### Body Talk

You cannot digest all the food you eat. Any waste passes through your large intestine, your **colon**, and your rectum and leaves your body as poop.

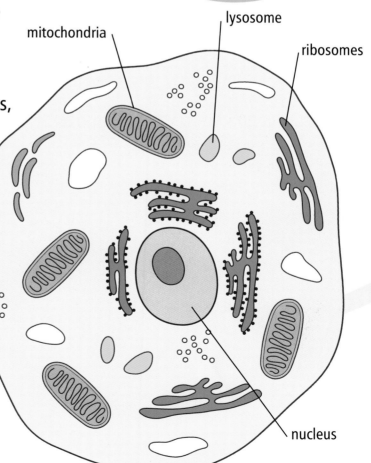

mitochondria

lysosome

ribosomes

membrane

nucleus

*Cells contain different structures. Each has a particular job to do. Vitamins help each structure play its role.*

# ADDING VITAMINS

Vitamin supplements can be dangerous. Children who think the vitamin supplement is a regular candy may eat too many. This could cause an overdose and can lead to serious health problems.

It is best to get the vitamins your body needs from food. But many people take supplements. Is this a good thing? It is for people who cannot get enough vitamins through healthy eating. It is bad if people use supplements to replace healthy eating.

## The dangers of supplements

Some vitamin supplements are sold as candies and gummies. This may make it easier for young children to get essential vitamins. However, it promotes unhealthy eating habits—the idea that you do not need to eat healthy foods, but simply chew on a candy to get the vitamins you need.

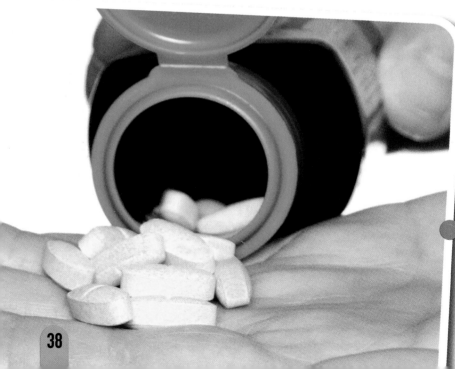

*Supplements can boost vitamin levels in the body.*

Instead of a supplement, get your vitamins from a fabulous fruit parfait.

## Try this...

### Did you know?

In 1935, a Swiss doctor named Tadeusz Reichstein successfully made vitamin C in a laboratory, creating the world's very first vitamin supplement.

### You will need:

1 cup (240 ml) of plain yogurt
1 tablespoon (15 ml) of honey
1 cup (240 ml) of mixed berries (blueberries, blackberries, raspberries, and strawberries)
½ cup (120 ml) of oat granola

### Instructions:

• Mix the yogurt with the honey.
• In the bottom of an ice cream glass or large glass, add two tablespoons (30 ml) of berries.
• Add four tablespoons (60 ml) of yogurt mixture.
• Add two tablespoons (30 ml) of granola.
• Repeat until you reach the top of the glass.

### Now eat your vitamins!

This recipe is easy to make and contains a lot of vitamins: vitamin K in blackberries; vitamin C in strawberries; vitamin E in blueberries and the nuts in the granola; folic acid in the raspberries, strawberries, blackberries, and oats; vitamin B12 in yogurt; and vitamin B5 in the oats. Enjoy!

## My food is rich!

Many vitamins are lost during food processing. Scientists have figured out ways to add vitamins to these foods to replace those that are lost. These are called enriched foods, and they include bread and pasta.

Bread and pasta are made with flour—a soft, fine powder made by grinding up cereal grains, especially wheat. Flour loses most of its vitamins when the grains are ground up. So food manufacturers add thiamine, riboflavin, niacin, and folic acid to the flour to enrich it.

## Fortified foods

Some foods even have extra amounts of vitamins added to them. This means they have more vitamins than they would normally contain. They are called **fortified** foods. Fortified foods include breakfast cereals, milk, soy drinks, and fruit juices.

*Breakfast cereals and bread are often fortified with vitamins and minerals to add important nutrients to your diet.*

## Body Talk

Body odor and bad breath can be gross! The conditions can be caused by many factors, including a lack of vitamin B.

## Did you know?

Some companies use the terms "enriched" or "fortified" to market their products as being very healthy. For example, cereal may be described as "fortified with essential vitamins." However, it may also contain a lot of sugar, which actually makes it an unhealthy choice.

## Starving for vitamins

People who do not get enough nutrients in their diets suffer from poor nutrition, or malnutrition. The World Health Organization (WHO) states that malnutrition is the biggest threat to public health. Every year, millions of children die of hunger.

More than half of the world's hungry people live in South Asia. The remaining 40 percent live in Africa and South America. One out of eight children under the age of 12 living in the United States goes to bed hungry. This problem is often treated by providing people with vitamin supplements and fortified foods.

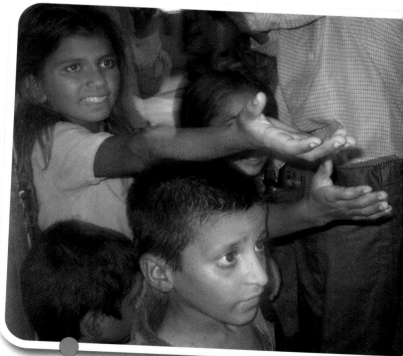

*Children in poor countries often do not get enough food, and so do not get enough vitamins.*

# SPECIAL DIETS

> I play a lot of sports, so I need extra vitamins and minerals to replace those lost through my sweat.

Everyone is different, so people need different amounts of nutrients to stay healthy. Children have special vitamin needs because their bodies are still growing and developing. Many children eat too much **processed** food, such as burgers and fries, so they are not getting enough vitamins.

As you now know, vitamin deficiencies can lead to serious health problems.

### Growing older

Older people need more vitamins and minerals to stay healthy. As people grow older, their bodies are less able to take in nutrients. Many seniors also need medications to stay healthy, and this also affects the intake of nutrients in the body.

*Vitamins are needed for healthy growth.*

## Body Talk

Some people think that taking lots of vitamin C helps to prevent common colds. In the winter, they may take vitamin C supplements to try to boost the level of vitamin C in the body. Unfortunately, this is a myth. your body cannot store vitamin C and uses only what it needs. Any extra vitamin C then leaves the body through your urine.

*Your body grows by making new cells. You cannot make healthy cells without vitamins.*

The bones become weaker as the body ages, so vitamin D is an important nutrient. It helps the body absorb calcium, which promotes strong bones. Other vitamins fight off harmful free radicals in the body. Free radicals are thought to be one of the main causes of cancer.

### Did you know?

Doctors think that a lack of vitamin K may contribute toward Alzheimer's disease. This illness affects the brain and leads to memory loss, dementia, and complete helplessness.

# FOOD FACTS AND STATS

Your body needs vitamins for many important body processes. Vitamins help us grow, make bones, fight infections, and heal wounds. They help us sense the world, and they even prevent us from bleeding to death.

**Recommended daily amounts of various vitamins**
*Note: 1 IU is equal to around 0.75 mg*

| | |
|---|---|
| Vitamin A | 4,000 IU/day ages 1–3; 5,000 IU/day ages 4–6; 7,000 IU/day ages 7–10; 8–10,000 IU/day ages 12 + |
| Vitamin B1 | Children need 0.6 to 0.9 mg |
| Vitamin B2 | Children need 0.6 to 0.9 mg |
| Vitamin B3 | Children need 9–16 mg |
| Vitamin B5 | Children need 2–4 mg |
| Vitamin B6 | Children need 0.6–1.3 mg |
| Vitamin B7 | *There is no recommended dietary allowance established for biotin. Adequate intakes are 8 mcg for 1–3 years; 12 mcg for 4–8 years; 20 mcg for 9–13 years |
| Vitamin B12 | Children need 0.9–2.4 mcg |
| Vitamin C | Children need 45–50 mg |
| Vitamin D | Children need about 5 mcg |
| Vitamin E | Children need 6–11 mg |
| Vitamin K | Children need 30–40 mcg |

| Vitamin | Fruits | Vegetables | Meat | Other |
|---|---|---|---|---|
| Vitamin A | cantaloupe, grapefruit, tomatoes, guavas, passion fruit, mangos, watermelons | spinach, carrots, broccoli, pumpkins | tuna fish | cream cheese, whipped cream, milk, eggs, sour cream, goat cheese, pecans, pistachios |
| B1 thiamine | mangos, oranges, pineapples, watermelons, avocados, dates, grapes | asparagus, corn, Brussels sprouts, okra, sweet potatoes, potatoes, peas | beef, pork, catfish, salmon, tuna, duck | cashews, flax seed, oats, peanuts, rye, wheat |
| B2 riboflavin | bananas, avocados, lychees, mangos, mulberries, pomegranates | artichokes, lima beans, pumpkins, broccoli, asparagus, mushrooms, Swiss chard | beef, chicken, pork, lamb, turkey | cheese, eggs, almonds, oats, buckwheat |
| B3 niacin | nectarines, loganberries, boysenberries, passion fruit, peaches, mangos, dates, avocados | peas, potatoes, pumpkins, butternut squash, parsnips, corn, mushrooms, sweet potatoes | beef, chicken, tuna, salmon, turkey, lamb, pork, sardines, herring, catfish | barley, rye, sunflower seeds, peanuts, spelt, wheat |
| B5 pantothenic acid | starfruit, guava, watermelons, avocados, blackcurrants, pomegranates | broccoli, corn, mushrooms, potatoes, parsnips, pumpkins | beef, chicken, pork, turkey, salmon, tuna, catfish | oats, rye, sunflower seeds, wheat, buckwheat milk, eggs, soy milk |
| B6 pyridoxine | bananas, avocados, gooseberries, grapes, watermelons, pineapples, mangos, dates | green peppers, broccoli, kale, butternut squash, peas, potatoes, sweet potatoes, okra | turkey, chicken, tuna, salmon, herring, cod, catfish, pork | walnuts, pistachios, pumpkin seeds, wheat, chestnuts |
| B7 biotin | bananas, papayas, avocados | carrots, sweet potatoes, Swiss chard | tuna, salmon, pork | eggs, milk, peanuts, almonds |
| B9 folic acid | raspberries, strawberries, blackberries, oranges, pineapples, papayas, guava, dates, avocados | spinach, asparagus, broccoli, Chinese cabbages, bok choy, parsnips, okra | salmon, lamb | cheese, eggs, soy beans, hazelnuts, oats, rye, sunflower seeds |
| B12 cyanocobalamin | none | none | shellfish, beef, salmon, tuna, lamb, pork | eggs, milk, cheddar cheese, cottage cheese, yogurt |
| Vitamin C | strawberries, oranges, pineapples, papaya, grapefruits, mangos, tomatoes | green and red peppers, broccoli, bok choy, potatoes, butternut squash | cod, perch | chestnuts, soy beans, yogurt |
| Vitamin D | none | mushrooms | beef, chicken | sunshine |
| Vitamin E | kiwis, peaches, papaya, grapes, cranberries, nectarines, raspberries, blueberries | taro, pumpkins, potatoes, parsnips | herring, sardines | almonds, hazelnuts, pine nuts, sunflower seeds |
| Vitamin K | kiwis, pears, cranberries, plums, tomatoes, pomegranates, mangos, blackberries, avocados | alfalfa sprouts, cabbages, carrots, celery, cauliflowers, leeks, spinach, broccoli, asparagus | beef, lamb, turkey, anchovies | eggs, cheese, cashews, pine nuts, rye |

# GLOSSARY

**antioxidant** Substance that mops up harmful products

**atom** Smallest part of an element that can exist alone

**bacteria** Very small living organisms made of only one cell

**calorie** Unit measuring the amount of energy a food will produce

**carbohydrate** Sugar or starch that is the main source of energy

**chyme** Digestive juice

**clot** The thickening and sticking together of a liquid to make a lump

**colon** Lower part of the bowels, where food is changed into waste

**deficiency** Lack of something

**diabetes** Disease in which the body lacks insulin, resulting in high levels of sugar in the blood

**esophagus** Muscular tube that runs from your throat to your stomach

**fat** Oily substance in food that provides energy

**fetus** Growing baby inside the uterus

**fortified** Added elements to improve the quality of food

**free radical** Harmful substance produced by body processes

**hormone** Chemical released by cells or glands that controls processes in other parts of the body

**immune system** System that makes your body fight against disease

**insulin** Hormone that controls how much sugar is in the blood

**intestine** Long tube in the body through which food passes after leaving the stomach

**lymph system** System that makes white blood cells that fight disease

**membrane** Thin layer of tissue that covers a surface

**molecule** Smallest part of a substance

**nutrient** Healthy source of nourishment

**organic** Coming about naturally; coming from nature

**process** To change or prepare food using several ingredients and other substances such as salt and chemicals

**protein** One of the main nutrients

**rectum** Lowest part of your bowels

**saliva** Watery mixture in the mouth

# FURTHER READING

## Further Reading

Sayer, Dr. Melissa, *Too Fat? Too Thin? The Healthy Eating Handbook*. Crabtree Publishing, 2009

Doeden, Matt, *Eat Right*. Lerner, 2009.

Gardner, Robert, *Health Science Projects about Nutrition*. Enslow Publishers, 2002.

Royston, Angela. *Vitamins and Minerals for a Healthy Body*. Heinemann-Raintree, 2009.

## Internet

Your Digestive System
http://kidshealth.org/kid/htbw/
    digestive_system.html

Learning about Vitamins
http://kidshealth.org/kid/
    stay_healthy/body/vitamin.html

Your Gross and Cool Body
http://yucky.discovery.com/
    flash/body/pg000126.html

## Try this...

Consider keeping a food journal. Write down everything you eat for an entire week. How much of each type of vitamin did you eat? Was it more or less than you needed? Which foods did they come from?

# INDEX